D0563572

The Funny Side of Tennis

Cal Samra
with 11 cartoonists

A publication of

The Joyful Noiseletter
funnysideoftennis.com

There are 24.7 million tennis players in the United States. If you are one of them, you are likely to see yourself and your tennis friends in this hilarious book of tennis cartoons, anecdotes, and witty quotes. If you're not one of them, this book is the perfect gift to cheer up a tennis player who needs some laughs.

But that's not all. This book is also about the health benefits of tennis played with good humor. "Laughter is good medicine," says Dr. Ellen Rome, a Cleveland Clinic physician who is a tennis player herself, "and if tennis is played for fun and with good humor, the health benefits are even greater."

Here's more proof that vigorous exercise and humor are powerful weapons in the never-ending battle against obesity and depression.

You'll read about the longevity of many tennis players, humorists, and comedians. And you'll be inspired by stories of tennis aficionados who play competitive amateur tennis into their eighties and nineties.

And you'll be introduced to Samra's Law: *The older tennis players get, the funnier they get.*

To cartoonist Bil Keane,
creator of The Family Circus –
a national treasure,
and to my own family circus,
who've given me more love
and laughs than I deserve.

©2008 by Cal Samra

All rights reserved. This book may not be reproduced in whole or in part, by any means, without written permission of the publisher. For information, address: Permissions, *The Joyful Noiseletter,* P.O. Box 895, Portage, MI 49085. Fax: (269) 324-3984. E-mail: JoyfulNZ@aol.com.

A publication of
The Joyful Noiseletter
www.funnysideoftennis.com

Composed and printed in the United States of America

Cover design: Teri Williams, Original Graphics, Kalamazoo, MI

ISBN 978-0-933453-02-9

10 9 8 7 6 5 4 3 2 1

Library of Congress Cataloging-in-Publication Data is available.

Mixed doubles is a great social game. Husbands and wives find hours of fun and togetherness playing mixed doubles.

"How old would you be if you didn't know how old you are? I know 20-year-old guys with 90-year-old minds, and 90-year-old guys with 20-year-old minds."

—Satchel Paige
(at age 48, still pitching
in the Major Leagues.)

Acknowledgments

Many of the cartoons in this book have been contributed by Bil Keane, creator of *The Family Circus* cartoons, which have had a huge and loyal following in 1,500 newspapers since 1960.

Keane, a lean and young 85, has had a lifelong love affair with tennis. He calls himself a "net-wit," who plays "semi-serious tennis."

"For years I have sat at the drawing board doing my syndicated cartoons, dressed in tennis clothes with my racquet at my side," Keane said. "Somebody just might phone and say, 'Let's play!' If work starts to interfere with tennis, the work has to go."

For years, Keane, his wife, Thel, and their five children could be found playing on their own court in Paradise Valley, Arizona, or on one of the many courts in the area. Ten years ago, while visiting the Keanes, my wife, Rose, and I played doubles with Bil and Thel on their home court, and were thoroughly vanquished in a good-humored way.

Keane has played against the likes of humorist Art Buchwald, *Peanuts* creator Charles Schulz, Jerry Van Dyke, NBC/ESPN tennis commentator Bud Collins, and Mike Blanchard, a referee at Forest Hills and official umpire at international events.

After playing with Keane, Blanchard commented, "Bil is funnier on the tennis court," and added, "In addition to being a great sport, tennis should be fun."

There were always lots of smiles and laughs when the Keanes played tennis. Keane, himself an experienced linesman and former USTA umpire, makes tennis and everything else he touches fun.

Keane's friend and neighbor, humorist Erma Bombeck, with whom he collaborated on a book titled *Just Wait Til You Have Children of Your Own,* occasionally dropped by to play tennis.

Keane and Erma's husband, Bill Bombeck, would regularly jog together. After watching them jogging, Erma wrote in her newspaper column: "The only reason I would take up jogging is so I could hear heavy breathing again."

Of the Bil Keane cartoons in this book, only one is a *Family Circus* cartoon. All the others are tennis cartoons drawn especially for his memorable book, *Deuce and Don'ts of Tennis,* published in 1975, which received kudos from many reviewers and became a bestseller.

We are most grateful to Bil Keane not only for his contributions to this book, but also for his friendship and wise counsel through the years.

For the *Peanuts* cartoons, we also appreciated the assistance of archivist Lisa Monhoff of the Charles M. Schulz Museum and Research Center in Santa Rosa, California, and United Feature Syndicate.

We thank, too, the other cartoonists who contributed to this book: Dennis Daniel, Bill Frauhiger, Jonny Hawkins, Dik LaPine, Ron Morgan, Tim Oliphant, Harley Schwadron, Wendell W. Simons, and Ed Sullivan. All of the cartoons in this book are reprinted by permission.

We also thank for their assistance the following officials of the United States Tennis Association: Joe Rasgado of Cooper City, Florida, a member of the International Committee of the United States Tennis Association; David Schobel, director of competitive play, and Theresa Bowen, coordinator of competitive play, at the USTA's national office in White Plains, New York; Dr. Ellen Rome, head of the Adolescent Medicine Section of the Cleveland Clinic and a member of the USTA's Sports Science Committee; and Dr. Gordon G. Blackburn, director of Cardiac Rehabilitation at the Cleveland Clinic.

We are also grateful to:

Vic Braden and Dave Nostrant, general manager of the Vic Braden Tennis College in St. George, Utah. Braden, who began his career at Kalamazoo College, is a well-known sports science researcher, psychologist, and television tennis commentator.

Deno Frier, general manager of Western Michigan University's West Hills Athletic Club in Kalamazoo, Michigan, and his cheerful and patient staff.

The many players who contributed anecdotes to this book.

The spirited friends I play doubles with regularly in the Kalamazoo/Portage tennis community and who put up with my clowning.

Terri Raich, our meticulous typesetter and design consultant.

And last, but surely not the least, my wife, Rose, and our sons, Luke, Paul, and Matt, my daughter-in-law Becky, and our grandchildren, Madeline, Kate, and Lizzie.

—**Cal Samra**

Introduction

The author of a book on tennis mentioned in his introduction that he had looked for tennis humor for years, with little success. One of our friends, Jim Reed of Cotter, Arkansas, has authored two books titled *The Funny Side of Golf* and *The Funny Side of Fishing*. Another friend, Joe Garagiola, recently authored a hilarious book titled *Just Play Ball!* – memories of his years as a major league catcher and Hall of Fame baseball sportscaster.

But tennis?

A sociology professor at Kalamazoo College – home of the famed USTA Boys 18 & 16 National Championships, which many famous pros played as teenage amateurs – told me he never heard anything funny about tennis in a half-century.

There are 24.7 million tennis players in America, according to the United States Tennis Association. If you are one of them, you are likely to see yourself – and laugh – somewhere in this book.

If you look for it, you'll find lots of humor and laughter among tennis players, especially among the older players.

Granted, professional tennis tends to be a super-serious sport. The pros, with few exceptions, play with a solemnity that suggests the Apocalypse might arrive with every serve.

Rarely, a glimmer of humor breaks through. At the U.S. Open in 2007, Novak Djokovic, the 20-year-old No. 3 seed, delighted the Arthur Ashe Stadium crowd and a national TV audience with hilarious impersonations of Maria Sharapova, Rafael Nadal, and Andy Roddick. This young court jester, the son of a fun-loving, close-knit Serbian family, went on to win the 2008 Australian Open.

In his later years as a player, Jimmy Connors clowned around on the court – to the delight of his many fans. Both Connors and John McEnroe have grown from the angry young men of tennis into mellow middle-aged humorists as coach and sportscaster. Andre Agassi also has displayed a warm sense of humor.

Years ago, Vic Braden, a professional tennis player himself, pioneered the use of humor in teaching and coaching tennis. Braden put together instructional books and videos like *Laugh and Win at Doubles,* with coauthor Bill Bruns, and strove to make tennis a fun sport at the Vic Braden Tennis College in St. George, Utah.

"Vic Braden has a great sense of humor," wrote Chris Evert. And Tracy Austin, recalling her days in Vic Braden's junior program in Palos Verdes, commented, "We worked unbeliev-ably hard, but we also laughed hard and we always had a lot of fun."

Humor thrives in the world of amateur tennis.

We are a family of tennis players. My wife, Rose, has won a state title with her travel team. My son, Luke, won a No. 1 state doubles championship with his state champion Hackett Catholic Central High School team in Kalamazoo. My son, Matt, played for a Kalamazoo Valley Community College team that won a regional title.

I've played amateur tennis for more than a half-century, and never won a tournament or a trophy. Those are the breaks – and maybe also the talent.

I've tried everything to improve my game – different racquets, different grips, different shoes, different coaches, etc.

I even tried grunting. You know you're getting old if you can remember when tennis players didn't grunt or scream when they hit the ball. The grunt in tennis was unknown until Monica Seles started grunting, or screaming, every time she hit the ball. Then other female pros started grunting, and some of the male pros took it up. So now most of the female and male pros are grunting when they hit the ball.

I tried grunting, but I still didn't win a tournament.

An unforgettable character named Lou Berman introduced me to the humor in tennis 25 years ago in Phoenix, Arizona. My health had greatly deteriorated, mainly because of a poor diet of mainly junk foods, a cigarette-smoking habit, a lack of exercise, and an excess of feeding on and reporting bad news. My family physician strongly advised me to resign my job as a newspaper reporter in Michigan and to go to the warmer climate of Arizona.

I arrived in Phoenix weighing about 103 pounds and looking like skin-and-bones. I was jobless and very depressed. A motel clerk suggested that if I wanted to play tennis, I should go down to Encanto Park, a city park in midtown Phoenix. There were a lot of tennis players looking for pickup games at Encanto, he said.

I met Lou Berman at a pickup game in Encanto Park. He was 73 then, but he had been playing tennis – good tennis – on two artificial hips for more than ten years, even though he was often in pain. He hobbled around the court and needed a faster, much younger player, like myself, to be his doubles partner.

We were an odd-couple doubles team. Lou was a merry-hearted Jewish businessman; I was an unemployed Greek Orthodox Christian.

We became friends. Lou was always cracking jokes and clowning around on and off the tennis court. He was fond of quoting Victor Borge: "A smile is the shortest distance between two people."

I played tennis almost every day in Phoenix, and the combination of the daily vigorous exercise, fresh air, sun, and laughter worked a miracle in my life. Slowly but steadily I regained my health, weight, and my good spirits.

I now play doubles regularly in a men's league that includes several medical doctors at Western Michigan University's West Hills Racquet Club in Kalamazoo. Many doctors of all medical disciplines are now saying that exercise and humor are powerful healing tools.

Dr. Ellen Rome, head of the Adolescent Medicine Section of the Cleveland Clinic, a member of USTA's Sports Science Committee, and a tennis player herself, told me:

"Tennis is a lifelong sport that you can play from toddler years to pre-nursing home. It can engage the whole family, and it doesn't involve a lot of expense.

"Mommy, why do we have so many trophies with lady tennis players on them and only one with a man on it?"

"It's great cardiovascular exercise. For healthy bodies and healthy minds, engaging in an activity such as tennis that gets you breaking a sweat for an hour – at whatever skill level you play – can combat obesity and generate that natural high that athletes and non-athletes crave.

"Laughter is also good medicine, and if tennis is played for fun and with good humor, the health benefits are even greater!"

Another tennis player, Dr. Gordon G. Blackburn, director of Cardiac Rehabilitation at the Cleveland Clinic, said that tennis, "can provide positive health benefits, including higher functional capacity, lower weight/body fat, and improved bone density. If a person engages in tennis frequently enough over a sufficient time period, they stand to gain health benefits."

In an age when obesity and depression have become epidemic, the health benefits of tennis are obvious. In tennis, just about every part of the body is exercised, and the mind is kept occupied on things other than self, symptoms, and worries.

We asked a lot of players, coaches, pros, and cartoonists: "What's the funniest thing you've ever experienced, seen, or heard on a tennis court?" Some of their answers are in this book.

The opinions expressed in this book are not necessarily the views of all the contributors.

Enjoy!

—**Cal Samra**

The over-90's gang

The USTA sponsors four national championships for men over-90 around the country, including hard court, clay, grass, and indoor tournaments. The USTA also recently added a competitive tennis division for women over 90.

In 2001, Emil Johnson, a former bacteriologist from Orlando, Florida, was ranked No. 1 in the 90's Super Seniors circuit. Dr. Johnson ran around the court like a teenager in his hard-fought singles match against Ken Beer, a retired 97-year-old pilot, at the hard court championships in Palm Springs, California.

Interviewed after the match, Dr. Johnson told *Wall Street Journal* reporter Bill Richards that two years earlier, he had had a heart attack, and his cardiologist warned him that he'd have to stop playing tennis.

"What did I do?" Johnson said. "I got another cardiologist."

"Here you are, Roger."

Pre-game alibis will make your opponent over-confident and give you adequate excuses to fall back on during the match.

"What a party last night! Didn't get into bed til three... Got any aspirin, Jim?"

A sin to play tennis on Sunday?

The conscience of an avid tennis player who plays in a Sunday men's league was troubled. He went to see his pastor about it.

"Pastor," the man asked, "is it a sin to play tennis on Sunday?"

"The way you play," the pastor, also a tennis player, replied, "it's a sin to play tennis on *any* day."

The ethics of tennis

Philosophy Professor Mike Pritchard, director of the Ethics Center at Western Michigan University, was playing doubles with a group of male friends. Pritchard was bent over at the net when his partner smashed the ball with a powerful forehand.

The ball struck Prof. Pritchard squarely in the *gluteal cleft* (the medical term for the cleavage in his behind) and stuck there, "long enough for our opponents to wonder where it went."

His partner graciously apologized.

Prof. Pritchard, of course, was philosophical about it.

"Thankyounicegame."

The *Peanuts* gang on the courts

Like his friend – cartoonist Bil Keane, Charles M. Schulz, creator of the enormously popular *Peanuts* comic strip, was a tennis enthusiast. He constructed both outdoor courts and indoor courts housed in a redwood structure next to his home in Santa Rosa, California.

These two giants of American cartooning occasionally played tennis together. "Sparky" Schulz was very athletic, and stayed fit and trim. His wife, Jeannie, also is an excellent tennis player.

From time to time in the *Peanuts* cartoons, Charlie Brown, Snoopy, Lucy, and Linus appeared playing tennis in their own inimitable way.

Jeannie Schulz said that Sparky loved to tell the following story: "When Sparky was about 60, he was playing in a local tournament in the 'C' division. He and his opponent, a young woman, were introduced, provided with a can of balls, and told to report to court three. On the way out to the court, the young woman said to Sparky, 'Oh, and you can't lob because I haven't had that lesson yet.'"

"If I were given the opportunity to present a gift to the next generation," Schulz once said, "it would be the ability to laugh at oneself."

It was also Schulz who said, "Don't worry about the world coming to an end today. It's already tomorrow in Australia."

PEANUTS: ©United Feature Syndicate, Inc.

PEANUTS: ©United Feature Syndicate, Inc.

PEANUTS: ©United Feature Syndicate, Inc.

The focused fanatic

While he and his doubles partner were engaged in a fiercely contested tennis match on the outdoor clay courts of the country club, a funeral procession appeared and moved slowly down the road past the tennis courts.

About to serve, the player stepped back, took off his cap, placed it over his heart, and bowed his head.

When the funeral procession passed, he put his cap back on, stepped up, and served an ace.

"Well, that funeral procession sure didn't interfere with your concentration," his partner said admiringly.

"It wasn't easy to keep my concentration," the man replied. "After all, we were happily married for 23 years."

A career employee at the Food and Drug Administration in Washington asked a coworker: "If, as they say, laughter is the best medicine, shouldn't we be regulating it?"

—Jim Reed
Cotter, AR

If you touch any part of the baseline before striking the ball while serving, it is a foot fault.

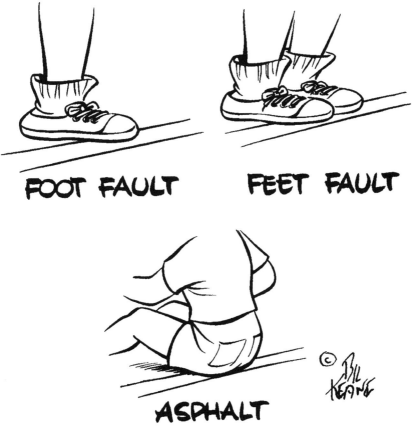

FOOT FAULT   FEET FAULT

ASPHALT

(Very difficult to do while serving.)

"I bought some No-Fault insurance because I thought it would help my serve."

—Bil Keane

'Micro-managing macho-men'

"My wife and I were playing a mixed doubles championship match in Palm Springs, California. The midday summer courtside temperature was 130 degrees.

"We offered our married opponents a chance to play a simple six-game pro set, winner take all. But the macho-man opponent wanted to play two out of three regular sets, and his reluctant wife yielded to his judgment.

"I wrapped ice-cubes around my wife's neck, suggested she drink a lot of water, and told her not to move. *I* would get everything.

"It did not work very well in the first set, and we lost it by a good margin. However, in the second set, macho-man's wife started to go downhill fast. She was cramping and nearly barfing. We won the second and third sets easily.

At the end, she was not even speaking to her husband.

"The last time my wife and I played mixed doubles, she dumped a tennis can of water on my head before a large crowd of country club spectators because, she said, I was 'micro-managing.'

"Lesson: It is only a tennis match. Take any reasonable offer to protect your partner! A marriage could well be hanging in the balance if you're playing mixed doubles with your wife."

—Jim Elsman, Esq.
Bloomfield Hills, MI

"YOURS!"

"*Wherever I travel, battle-scarred women from mixed doubles invariably want to know, 'What should I do about a partner who tries to hog all the shots? He thinks he's better than he actually is, so he tries to play the whole court, and that spoils the fun for me…' I advise them: Tell him, 'Look, it's not much fun for me when you try to take all the shots. I'm not really playing doubles here. I'm watching you play singles, so we have to talk this out.*"

—Vic Braden

PEANUTS: ©United Feature Syndicate, Inc.

PEANUTS: ©United Feature Syndicate, Inc.

"How's your lob?"

An earthshaking match

Betsy Kuhle, the high-energy women's tennis coach at Western Michigan University, is WMU's longest-tenured coach in any sport. A rare accomplishment in these days of revolving doors for coaches.

In 25 years, she's led her women' tennis team to ten Mid-American Conference championships. But she also strives to prepare them for life without tennis.

"I want them to be competitors," Kuhle says. "I have learned that the will to compete comes back to you when you need it – when you find out that you have breast cancer, when your boss tells you you're fired. It comes back when bad things happen and you learn to stand up on your own. A person who can't fight won't make it."

An example of Kuhle's competitiveness:

She and a friend were playing doubles in La Jolla, California, against Bob Hagey and his son, Chico, who had won the 16's in the Boys Nationals earlier. Just as Bob Hagey was serving, a mild earthquake struck the area and Hagey's first serve hit the net.

When the tremors stopped and play resumed, "Hagey wanted to get a let on his first serve," Kuhle laughed, "but we made him hit the second serve."

A birdie

Wally Sims, the former editor of the *Enquirer & News* in Battle Creek, Michigan, was playing doubles in a fiercely competitive match at the Battle Creek Country Club. As his partner served, a sparrow flew over the net. The tennis ball struck and killed the bird.

"Our opponents refused to give us a let," Sims said.

"*We've all played against the team that suffers from 'out-itis,' a compulsive tendency to call 'out' on all close line shots by their opponents… Unfortunately, there's not much you can do about players like this. You might simply say to the cheater, 'I'm disappointed with the way you call lines, and I'll simply hold up the number of fingers for the times I think you've hooked me.'*"

—Vic Braden

It isn't considered good sportsmanship to continually question your opponent's "out" calls, but sometimes a subtle look will get the message across.

'Treinta-cuarenta!'

This is one of Vic Braden's favorite tennis stories:

"In 1967 in Guayaquil, Ecuador, Cliff Richey was competing against Pancho Guzman in the first Davis Cup match of the day. During one game, Cliff heard the score called 'treinta-cuarenta' – 30-40.

"Cliff said, 'No, it's 40-30' and the umpire replied, 'I didn't say anything!'

"After some very confusing conversation between the umpire and the players, a spectator yelled from the stands, 'It was the bird!'

"I ran down behind the stand with my camera, and sure enough, there was a giant parrot calling out, 'treinta-cuarenta!'

"The parrot, who lived next to the courts, was perched on a rubber tree branch. He would soar up, and when he got above the stands, he would call out the score. I always wondered why the bird only called 30-40 and never deuce."

©Jonny Hawkins

The trials of a tennis teaching pro

Deno Frier, general manager of Western Michigan University's West Hills Athletic Club in Kalamazoo, passed on these anecdotes he experienced as a teaching pro:

"An adult student came to me for her first lesson. As I started out feeding her some balls, I noticed that her racquet kept slipping in her hand on every shot.

"So I approached the net and told her that the first thing we have to do is to replace the grip on her racquet, as it must be worn badly because it keeps slipping.

"She replied that the grip can't possibly be worn because it was a brand new racquet and had never been used. It was then that I noticed that she hadn't taken the plastic cover off the grip."

"I taught at another tennis club where many of the members were research scientists with Ph.Ds. In a typically scientific way, they always seemed to want *precise* information about everything. For instance, "what degree angle do you hold the racquet for every shot?" "What angle do you launch the ball over the net?" "At what precise point do we abort the serve?"

"Another Ph.D. wanted to know what type of racquet I would recommend for him. Being sponsored by Wilson, I gave him my sales pitch on Wilson racquets. Then I discovered that he had already researched the Internet and had extensive information on practically every style of racquet made and their prices. He showed me five pages of computer printouts and seemed to be very disappointed at my limited knowledge as a teaching pro."

"If you're practicing lobbing you're doing great."

Invocation delivered by Rev. George Tribou at the American zone finals of the Davis Cup tennis matches:

"Lord, grant to the referee, the linesmen, and the umpires sharpness of vision and fairness of judgment that they may see from the sides with the same clarity with which You will be watching from above."

"When will his mommy lift him down
out of that high chair?"

"Could we play a let on that? I wasn't ready."

The serenity of silence

Dr. Ken Dorner, a Kalamazoo plastic surgeon, was playing doubles at Hilton Head Island in South Carolina on a tennis court next to a swimming pool. A portable radio was blaring at the swimming pool, which greatly annoyed one of Dorner's opponents.

A shouting match ensued between the opponent and the owner of the radio. After a heated argument, Dorner's opponent suddenly went ballistic, ran off the court, and up to the swimming pool.

Within a minute, there was dead silence, and our opponent returned to the court. "Well, that settles that," he said.

"How did you get him to turn off the radio?" we asked.

"Simple," he said. "I threw the radio in the pool."

The game continued in serene silence.

"Mommy! Marky's tinkling off the diving board!"

THREE WAYS TO PICK UP A TENNIS BALL

THE RAT-A-TAT-TAT METHOD
Used by the big guys
(pros and A players).

THE FOOT LIFT
Used by B
players.

STOOPID STYLE
Used by the
rest of us.

©Bil Keane

"*Fifty percent of the people who play tennis on a given day will lose. But everybody wins if you know how to have fun and enjoy the game. When you play with this philosophy, the winner has fun, plus he wins; the loser still has fun. He gets one out of two, and that's worth something in our win-at-all costs society.*"

—Vic Braden

"Rose, the girls are still buzzing over that great 'get' you made before you crashed into the pole!"

©Dennis Daniel

"What do you mean you've decided to settle out of court?"

©Jonny Hawkins

BIGFOOT SAID HE MISSED PLAYING 3RD SINGLES
ON HIS HIGH SCHOOL TENNIS TEAM.

©Ed Sullivan

"You won!"

©Harley L. Schwadron

"Marv, as your friend and doubles partner,
I advise you not to let it get you down.
I'm not mentioned on Google either."

"Fred, one of your doubles partners
tells me you're going bald."

©Bill Frauhiger

Horace is a lousy tennis player, but a great philosopher.

©Dennis Daniel

"You might want to get your racquet restrung."

©Jonny Hawkins

"So we lost again. At least we'll never get accused of taking steroids."

©Dennis Daniel

"Tennis bum."

©Jonny Hawkins

"Surely you have grounds for divorce other than your incompatibility as mixed doubles partners."

©Dennis Daniel

"I'm glad to hear your behavior has improved on the tennis court, Mr. Ludwig. I'm hiking my fee to see if you can handle it."

©Harley L. Schwadron

After 4 hours of back and forth action, it occurs to
Lars that perhaps he's in the wrong place.

©Jonny Hawkins

Federer Express

At the Australian Open, Roger Federer was making some amazing passing shots and beating Andy Roddick handily. After another Federer passing shot, a frustrated Roddick picked up the ball and hit it far out of the stadium. The ESPN sportscaster remarked dryly, "He's probably expecting Federer to get that one back, too."

"A wife watched her husband play tennis and told a friend, 'He's getting in shape. He doesn't turn purple until the second set now!' "

—Milton Berle

Middle-age is when you are too young to take up golf and too old to rush up to the tennis net."

—Franklin P. Adams

"May I approach the bench, your honor?"

©Dik LaPine

"What I *said* was... I'm into Alfred Lord Tennyson."

©Jonny Hawkins

"You need to take a break from
watching too many tennis matches."

©Tim Oliphant

Hitting the head that feeds you

While vacationing at a northern Michigan resort with his family, Political Science Professor Peter Kobrak, chair of the School of Public Affairs & Administration at Western Michigan University, took his young son, Harry, out to play tennis.

On the tennis court, two unknown gentlemen invited Kobrak and his son to play doubles. During the game, Harry hit a hard overhead smash that struck one of the unknown gentlemen squarely in the head.

"After the game, we introduced ourselves more formally," Kobrak said, "and it turned out that Harry had hit the chair of the Michigan House Education Appropriations Subcommittee, which has a lot to say about WMU's budget. I apologized profusely for Harry's hit, and afterwards, Harry and I played singles."

"My wife loves tennis and anything else that calls for an argument."

—Milton Berle

"You again, Grabowski?"

©Dennis Daniel

The cusser

Badly beaten in a singles match, a tennis player swore profusely, smashed his racquet on the court, and yelled: "I've got to give it up!"

"Give up tennis?" his opponent asked.

"No," he said, "give up the ministry."

Question: Where is tennis first mentioned in the Bible?

Answer: Joseph served in Pharoah's court.

—Rev. Dr. F. Christopher Anderson
York, PA

"Can't you ever take a day off? Other pastors do."

©Wendell W. Simons

RANKED NUMBER 276 IN THE WORLD, TENNIS PRO JOHN DOPPLER SEARCHES FAR AND WIDE FOR A GURU WHO WILL HELP HIM IMPROVE HIS GAME.

©Harley L. Schwadron

Matilda was nervous about the new ball retriever.

©Jonny Hawkins

The mantra

"One of my high school tennis coaches had the same advice when any of his players were getting beat. His mantra: 'Hit to the backhand!'

"I was having a very tough match against a very good, hard-hitting player. I asked my coach what I was doing wrong, and he told me, 'Hit to his backhand!'

"So I kept hitting to his backhand until it finally dawned on me that the guy didn't have a backhand – he was ambidextrous, and equally good with both hands. He beat me with both hands."

—Luke Samra
Portage, Michigan

"Forget about your losses. Laugh and hit. You'll have more fun and win more in the long run."

—Vic Braden

"Yes, sweetie, I know love is a good thing and makes the world go around, but in tennis, it means we haven't scored yet."

©Dennis Daniel

'Who, me?'

A 300-pound man took up tennis to lose weight. He was making progress and beginning to lose weight. But one day during practice, he stopped, sat down, and breathing heavily, told the club pro: "My brain gives orders to my body: 'Run! Hit the ball! Stop! Go back! Lob! Watch your grip on your backhand! And then my body replies, 'Who, me?'"

Sister Maria

Maria Sharapova, after being booed continually by fans rooting for her opponent during a match at the French Open:

"It's tough playing tennis and being Mother Teresa at the same time and making everyone happy."

**BERT CONSIDERS TREATMENT OPTIONS FOR
VARIOUS PAINS AND AFFLICTIONS HINDERING
HIS TENNIS GAME.**

©Harley L. Schwadron

Foolery

Two men were playing a serious game of social tennis one Saturday afternoon. It began raining heavily. They continued with their vigorous game when a light aircraft flew overhead.

One player said to the other, "Look at that fool up there! Fancy flying in this weather!"

—Rev. Bruce Raymond
Bulimba Uniting Church
Queensland, Australia

"They called Yogi Berra a bad ball hitter, but he said, 'It ain't bad if I hit it.'"

—Joe Garagiola
in *Just Play Ball*

"It's sort of a retro sports drink... it's called water."

©Ron Morgan

"I'm sorry, George. Love means nothing to me."

©Harley L. Schwadron

"I know all there is to know about tennis
except how to hold the bat."

"A sense of humor is one of the common characteristics displayed by players who are always in demand as doubles players."

—Vic Braden

"Never criticize, nag, or razz a teammate."

—Coach John Wooden

"My partner – er, my client would like to settle this matter out of court – er, off the court."

©Dik LaPine

"Doctor, he's at it again!"

©Tim Oliphant

The guys, gals and geezers of Encanto Park

Encanto Park in Phoenix is an enchanting city park full of palm trees, the fragrant aroma of orange trees, and free tennis courts. The players came in all sizes, shapes, and ages. There were a lot of jobless players like myself. There were wheelchair players. There were Hispanic-Americans and African-Americans. You didn't know it at the time, but there were also rich businessmen and women who came there incognito for the camaraderie and good-humored fellowship of the pickup games.

And there were a lot of retired seniors – men and women, some in their 70s and 80s – whose slowness afoot had long since forced them to change their strategy to baffle their opponents with a cut-and-spin placement game. They had a whole arsenal of trick shots and bizarre angles.

And most all of them had a keen sense of humor. Encanto Park was known for its congeniality and hospitality. If you were a stranger, like myself, and you sat on a bench and watched a doubles game, it wouldn't be long before a player would graciously drop out and invite you to play in his or her place.

My new friend Lou Berman had been attracted to the Valley of the Sun partly because, he said, "it has more tennis players than coyotes, roadrunners, and rattlesnakes; there are tennis leagues for everyone; and the women outnumber the men eight to one."

Lou had also come to Phoenix from Michigan, years earlier, and the first thing he said to me was, "I've seen a lot of guys

"George has become a real tennis bum."

©Dennis Daniel

drive down to Phoenix in $60,000 Cadillacs and drive back in $500,000 Greyhound buses."

Until I met Lou, I had taken tennis – and life – far too seriously. Lou and his wife invited me to dinner at their home, and the first thing he did was take me into his large backyard to show me his orange and grapefruit trees. Hanging from a couple dozen fruit trees were numerous broken and smashed tennis racquets.

He explained that he had broken them all in anger over the last 55 years, and had hung them in the trees to remind himself that anger hadn't helped his game.

Lou sometimes would reach back into the centuries-old wisdom of his faith to quote Proverbs 17:22 – "A cheerful heart is a good medicine, but a downcast spirit dries up the bones."

Lou had been playing tennis for decades, ever since he played on his high school tennis team in Michigan. And even though it was often painful to play on his two artificial hips, he just wouldn't quit.

"When I go, I want to go on a tennis court," he would say And that sentiment was echoed by many of the seniors at Encanto Park.

Lou was full of surprises, and one day he surprised me when he invited me to play doubles at the Arizona Biltmore, the luxurious resort and spa in Phoenix that was a world away from Encanto Park. This beautiful hotel-resort, whose design had been inspired by Frank Lloyd Wright, had eight swimming pools and attracted "celebrities, the rich and the famous."

We played tennis on several occasions at the Biltmore, where Lou was treated deferentially. He never told me, but I later found out that he was on the board of the Biltmore's Tennis Association.

Lou's unfailing cheerfulness, keen sense of humor, kindness, and courage were a great inspiration to me. Like the tennis racquets broken in anger and hung on his orange trees, he encouraged me to put away and hang up my own angers and fears, reignited my sense of humor, and helped me on the road back to good health.

My senior friends at Encanto Park were living proof for Norman Cousins' belief in the healing power of humor. We were all greatly amused by Lou's regular trek to play tennis with the poor and unemployed at Encanto Park, and then to play tennis with the "celebrities, rich, and famous" at the Biltmore.

Jas Davidson, long-time tennis director at the Arizona Biltmore, says she has heard that Lou Berman has gone to the Big Tennis Court in the Sky. I wish he were still here to enjoy the humor and cartoons in this book.

©Ron Morgan

"People hardly ever play the way they warm up, so don't let yourself be easily filled with boundless optimism or unbridled gloom… Laugh off the attempted 'psych' jobs. A player who attempts to psych out his opponents is usually a person who lacks all the weapons he needs to beat them straight."

—Vic Braden

Senior tennis players proliferate

The number of seniors, men and women, playing tennis is growing, according to Joe Rasgado, a member of the USTA's International Committee.

"Those 90-year-olds are unbelievable," Rasgado said. "A lot of them have hearing problems, and some don't remember the score good. They have to be told what the score is. They're competitive and they like to win, but it's not important who wins – they're just having fun."

A total of 865 male and female tennis players qualified for the 2007 Summer National Senior Games tennis tournament in Louisville, Kentucky, after 300 local competitions around the country. The Senior Olympians included three men who played in the 95-99 age group – Roger Gentilhomme, 98, of Florida; James Kales of Michigan, and Clarence Sinnette of West Virginia.

Some players didn't start playing tennis until their sixties. John Lyster, a fruit and dairy farmer in Bangor, Michigan, started playing tennis at age 64, and later won several trophies. After surgery for a severe knee injury a couple years ago, Lyster, now 85, returned to the courts wearing a brace, but as competitive as ever.

Another senior with a keen sense of humor, Sidney Tanoff, age 89, plays tennis three times a week in a retiree's league at West Hills. A U.S. Army veteran, Tanoff survived the Battle of the Bulge in World War II.

The senior tennis players are survivors. Many of them have to seek medical treatment for tennis elbow, rotator cuff injuries, knee injuries, ankle sprains, stress-fractures of the foot, plantar fascitis, etc. But more often than not, they battle back from these injuries.

Alan Messer of Toledo, Ohio, is an avid tennis player and a chair umpire and referee for the Men's International Professional Tennis Council. In January, 2004, he had a quintuple bypass, and after his recovery resumed playing tennis. Now 73, he is currently ranked 18th nationally in the men's 70's division.

He also recently developed a web site for "superseniors" for players 55 or older, listing about 600 upcoming tournaments, which receives more than 1,000 hits weekly.

Another senior, John Powless of Madison, Wisconsin, is secretary and newsletter editor of Super Senior Tennis, Inc., a not-for-profit group that promotes tennis competition for players ages 55 and over. Since 1949, SST also has promoted friendly, competitive tennis matches between American and Canadian veterans who met during World War II. The tournaments are still played annually every summer in alternating homelands.

In 2008, Les Dodson, 71, and Jack Vredevelt, 75, both of Kalamazoo, won their third consecutive 70's doubles title in the USTA's Florida Super Senior Grand Prix at the St. Petersburg Tennis Center. Dodson is a retired teacher and tennis coach at the Kalamazoo Y. Vredevelt is a former tennis coach at Vanderbilt and at Western Michigan University.

And they did it in spite of the fact that two years earlier, Dodson had knee surgery and was given two metal replacement knees.

On match point in the final set, Dodson fell flat on his back while going back to retrieve a lob. One of his opponents tried to hit him with the ball while he was down, but missed, and the Kalamazoo team won.

At a seniors mixed-doubles tournament in Germany, one of the male players collapsed on the court. An ambulance was called. While waiting for the ambulance, the stricken player asked a very pretty tennis player if she would sit with him and hold his hand, Dodson recalled. He died of an apparent heart attack before the ambulance arrived.

Dodson said, "All of the male players agreed before resuming play – 'What a way to go – dying on a tennis court with a pretty tennis player holding your hand!'"

A senior moment

While playing doubles in Kalamazoo, four seniors took a water break and exchanged some pleasantries. The friendly chitchat continued while they walked back to the court to resume their game.

"We had all taken our places and the server was preparing to serve to me when he suddenly stopped short," recalled one senior, who chose to remain anonymous. "I was standing there without my racquet, and he called my name and asked me to get my racquet, which I had left on the chair. A humbling moment in one's life."

My kingdom for a tennis shirt

An 88-year-old man signed up to play in the seniors doubles flight in the Kalamazoo Open at Stowe Stadium. On the hot tournament day in July, he showed up, picked up his tournament shirt, and then left the stadium without a word, leaving his partner and opponents mystified on the court.

His partner ran after him and begged him to return.

"Nah," he replied. "I just wanted to get one of those fancy tournament shirts they give out."

When some seniors play tennis in the over-90's.

©Dik LaPine

Seniors who refuse to retire

Seniors everywhere are showing a keen interest in physical fitness and nutrition, and becoming active in all kinds of sports. Waldo McBurney of Quinter, Kansas, is a 104-year-old, unretired beekeeper who at age 97 won the 200-meter dash in the Senior Olympics.

He took up long-distance racing at the age of 65. He credits his longevity to a sense of humor, a healthy natural diet, and a lifestyle full of physical activity. A lifelong gardener, he grows and eats over 30 different fresh fruits, vegetables, herbs, and whole grains.

McBurney recently authored a book titled *My First 100 Years! A Look Back from the Finish Line* (Leathers Publishing). "Motion," says McBurney, "is the best lotion."

Though McBurney eats very modest portions of some meats, his natural diet is very similar to the diet of TV fitness guru Jack La Lanne, a raw-food vegan who is still going strong at age 92 and who still works out in the gym for two hours every morning.

(Author's note: My nutrition-minded family physician suggests another important factor in my recovery from poor health – I returned to the Mediterranean diet my mother raised me on – lots of salads, fresh vegetables and fruits, whole grains, fish and cheese.)

TENNIS AFICIONADO MORT SCHMIDT SEEKS
PROFESSIONAL ADVICE ON THE BEST
DIET TO IMPROVE HIS GAME.

©Harley L. Schwadron

Good news and bad news

Two 80-year-old women, Sue and Barb, had loved playing tennis together all their lives, starting in high school.

When Sue was hospitalized and told by the doctors that she was dying, Barb visited her and said, "Sue, we've been good friends all these years. Please do me one favor: when you get to Heaven, somehow you must let me know if there's tennis there."

Sue replied, "If it's at all possible, I'll do this favor for you, my dear friend."

A couple weeks after Sue died, Barb was awakened one night by a blinding flash of light and a voice calling out, "Barb! Barb! It's me, Sue. I'm in Heaven. And I have some really good news for you and some bad news."

"Tell me the good news first," Barb said.

"The good news," Sue said, "is that there's tennis in Heaven. And all of our old friends who've died are here, too. We're all young again. It's always springtime. It never rains or snows. And best of all, we can play tennis all we want, and we never get tired."

"That's fantastic!" Barb replied. "It's beyond my wildest dreams! So what's the bad news?"

"You're playing here Tuesday," Sue said.

—via Theresa Bowen & David Schobel
USTA, White Plains, NY

"Dearie, my doctor told me 50 years ago that they don't race horses after a certain age, and warned me to quit playing tennis. He died two years later. Will you be my doubles partner in the over-90s tournament?"

©Dennis Daniel

On the longevity of comedians & humorists

've become intrigued by the longevity of comedians and humorists. Bob Hope and George Burns, who resurrected his comedy career at age 79, both lived to 100.

Here is a list of some other long-lived comedians and humorists and their ages: Steve Allen (78), Lucille Ball (78), Jack Benny (80), Milton Berle (93), Yogi Berra (83), Victor Borge (91), Vic Braden (79), Art Buchwald (80), Carol Burnett (75), Red Buttons (85), Johnny Carson (79), who once remarked, "Death is nature's way of giving someone else your tennis court," Charlie Chaplin (88), Bill Cosby (71), who observed that "the serve in tennis was invented so that the net can play, "Jimmy Durante (87), Joe Garagiola (82), Ernie Harwell (90), Bil Keane (85), Harold Lloyd (78), Groucho Marx (87), Malcolm Muggeridge (87), Satchel Paige (76), Martha Raye (78), Charles M. Schulz (77), George Bernard Shaw (100), Red Skelton (84), Danny Thomas (77), Mark Twain (75), Henny Youngman (92).

Interviewed by the *Journal of Longevity*, Red Buttons credited his longevity to "humor, health foods, and staying physically and mentally active." He added: "Eighty is not old. Old is when your doctor no longer X-rays you; he just holds you up to the light."

Steve Allen, the host of the original "Tonight Show," was one of my favorite comedians, and I had the privilege of meeting him and corresponding with him on several occasions.

When Allen was hospitalized briefly in 1986, he told a reporter his condition was critical – "critical of nurses, critical of doctors, critical of the food, critical of the prices."

Some, though not all, of these comedians and humorists were tennis players. Others were into golf, but all of them remained physically active into their senior years and retained a humorous and positive attitude towards life.

I agree with Dr. Ellen Rome of the Cleveland Clinic that if tennis is played for fun and with good humor, the health benefits are even greater.

In their book *Welcome to Your Brain,* scientists Sandra Aamoldt and Sam Wang report that exercise is strongly associated with a reduced risk of dementia late in life. My children and grandchildren may dispute that.

"Time out!"

©Wendell W. Simons

Samra's Law

I suspect Lou Berman would agree with what, in all humility, I will call Samra's Law. I say in all humility because tennis can be humbling, as the defeats, injuries, and ailments pile up as one ages. (The words "humor" and "humility" have the same Latin root – *humus*, "of the earth.")

Samra's Law:

Tennis players, with some exceptions, develop a sense of humor in direct proportion to their advancing age. The older tennis players get, the funnier they get.

"Don't be fooled by Rick's racquet face.
He's no Mr. Nice Guy on the court."

©Dennis Daniel

"Oh no, sweetie. I don't play. I just want to look like I do."

©Tim Oliphant

'Never, never, never, never give up!' – Churchill

"I was playing Gordy Nichol of Philadelphia in the men's 70's singles division at the Houston Indoor Championships in 2007. I won the first set, and led the second set by a seemingly insurmountable 5-0.

"Gordy did not give in, and soon had the score even at 5-5; then, he won 7-6, and mentally, I was toast for the third set.

"Along the way, I had fifteen match-points (*fifteen!*) but was never able to convert one for the match. I am not proud of it, but Gordy and I are still laughing about it.

"Lesson: Never relax and assume you control the future of a match. Strange things can happen, against the odds."

—Jim Elsman, Esq.
Bloomfield, Hills, Michigan

©Jonny Hawkins

©*The Joyful Noiseletter*

"Kilroy was here" was the famous graffiti spread all over the world by American GI's during World War II and the Korean war. Maybe you've sometimes spotted his cousin, Killjoy, on the other side of the net. Laugh him off.

"*Unfortunately, too many people bring that 'winning is the bottom line' philosophy not only to tennis, but to other individual and team sports — both as participants and as spectators. Yet I will continue to campaign on behalf of my belief that the laughing can even come before the winning, because that's still what sports should be about: Play as hard and as well as you can and have fun doing it; the winning will fall into place.*

"*A better game of tennis can coexist with laughter, and it should. Have fun, laugh your head off, and try to learn along the way.*"

—Vic Braden

"Keep runnin' and don't look back, because some-body might be gainin' on you."

—Satchel Paige

About the author

Humorist Cal Samra and his wife, Rose – longtime tennis aficionados – have authored ten humor/cartoon books on various topics that have sold nearly a million copies in the past decade. The Samras also have been editors of an award-winning humor newsletter for the past 23 years.

Samra is a former reporter for the Associated Press and newspapers in Michigan, New York, and New Jersey. He is the former lay executive director of the Huxley Institute, a psychiatric research foundation, but does not consider himself an authority on various forms of madness – except for amateur tennis.

The Samras live in Portage, Michigan, with their family circus and their serene and good-natured Golden Retriever, Maize, whose favorite bumper sticker is: "My Golden Retriever is smarter than your honor student."

The Funny Side of Tennis is available for $8.95 plus shipping charges from our toll-free number: 1-800-877-2757.

www.funnysideoftennis.com

The Funny Side of Tennis is a work in progress. We invite readers to send us the funniest things they've seen, heard, or experienced on a tennis court for a possible sequel to this book. Please send the anecdotes to Tennis Humor, P.O. Box 895, Portage, MI 49081-0895, or to JoyfulNZ@aol.com. Thank you.